ON THE WATER

Sailing

by Rachel Grack

BLASTOFF! READERS, AN IMPRINT OF BELLWETHER MEDIA BY FLUTTERBEE

Blastoff! Readers are carefully developed by literacy experts to build reading stamina and move students toward fluency by combining standards-based content with developmentally appropriate text.

Level 1 provides the most support through repetition of high-frequency words, light text, predictable sentence patterns, and strong visual support.

Level 2 offers early readers a bit more challenge through varied sentences, increased text load, and text-supportive special features.

Level 3 advances early-fluent readers toward fluency through increased text load, less reliance on photos, advancing concepts, longer sentences, and more complex special features.

★ **Blastoff! Universe**

Reading Level

Blastoff! Beginners — Grade K

Blastoff! Readers — Grades 1–3

Blastoff! Discovery — Grade 4

This edition first published in 2027 by Bellwether Media, Inc.

For information regarding permission, write to Bellwether Media, Inc., Attention: Permissions Department, 3500 American Blvd W, Suite 150, Bloomington, MN 55431.

Library of Congress Cataloging-in-Publication Data

Names: Koestler-Grack, Rachel A., 1973- author
Title: Sailing / by Rachel Grack.
Description: Blastoff! readers. | Minneapolis, Minnesota : Bellwether Media, Inc, [2027] | Series: On the water | Includes bibliographical references and index. | Audience: Ages 5-8 | Audience: Grades 2-3 | Summary: "Relevant images match informative text in this introduction to sailing. Intended for students in kindergarten through third grade" – Provided by publisher.
Identifiers: LCCN 2026013813 (print) | LCCN 2026013814 (ebook) | ISBN 9798898800598 (library binding) | ISBN 9798898801830 (ebook)
Subjects: LCSH: Sailing | LCGFT: Juvenile literature
Classification: LCC GV811.13 .K64 2027 (print) | LCC GV811.13 (ebook) | DDC 797.124–dc23/eng/20260325
LC record available at https://lccn.loc.gov/2026013813
LC ebook record available at https://lccn.loc.gov/2026013814

Editor: Kieran Downs Series Designer: Josh Brink Designer: Laura Sowers

Printed in the United States of America, North Mankato, MN.

Table of Contents

Wind-powered Boats

Sailing is the sport of using sailboats. The boats use sails to catch wind to move across water.

People sail on lakes, rivers, and oceans.

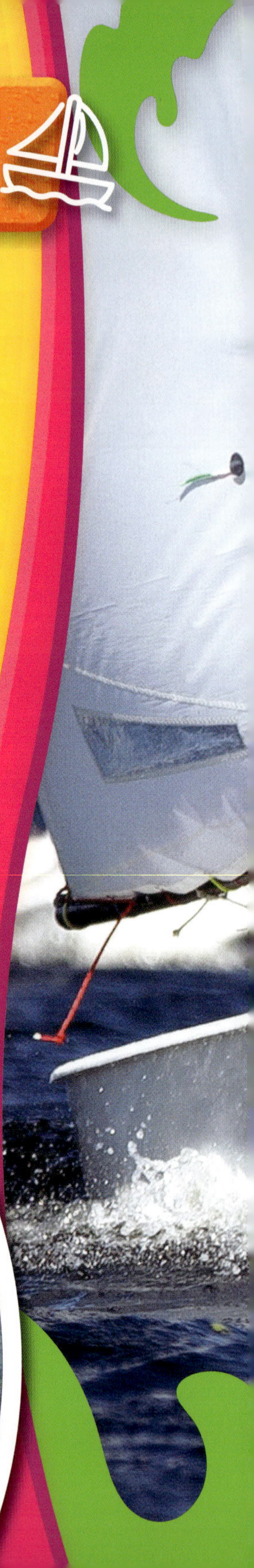

Top Place to Sail

Newport, Rhode Island, United States

Sailboats have many shapes and sizes. Beginners often use **dinghies**. These boats are small and light.

Cruisers are popular for longer sailing trips. Many cruisers have cabins.

Sailboats have different types of sails. The mainsail drives the boat forward.

The headsail works with the mainsail for **balance**. Ropes control the sails and **rigging**.

Sailors wear gloves to help them hold ropes. They carry a horn and **flares** in case of trouble.

They bring life jackets
and first aid supplies.

What Sailors Need

Getting Started on Sailing

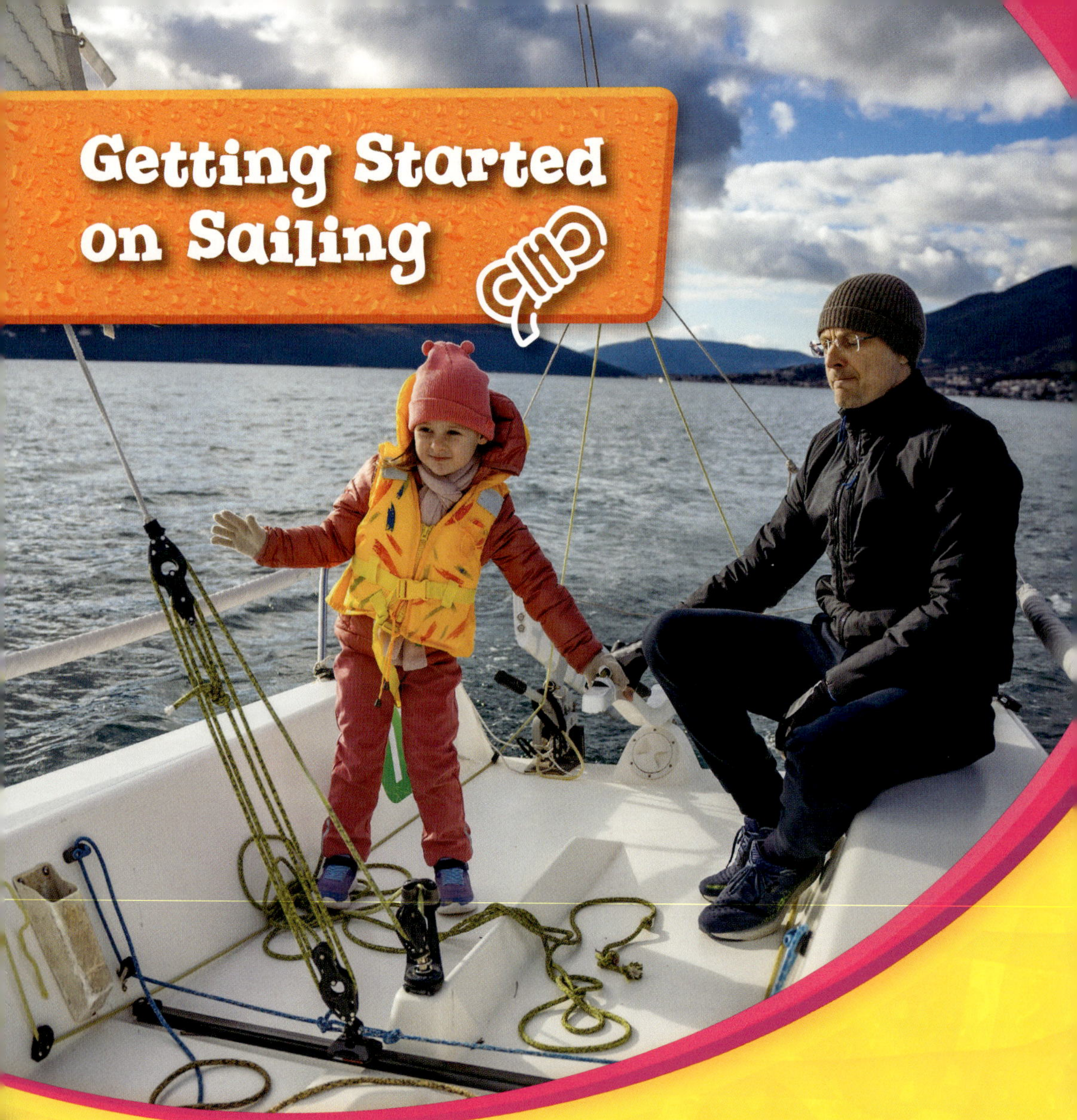

Sailing takes training and practice. Most people take lessons.

Sailors learn how to **rig** a sailboat. They practice keeping the boat steady.

Sailors read the wind direction. Some use **navigation** tools. Others look for ripples in the water.

They find the **points of sail**.

Sailors use a **rudder** to turn the boat. A handle controls the rudder's direction.

Sailors push it left or right. The boat turns in the opposite direction.

Sailors **trim** the sails to guide the boat. They tighten the ropes to **tack**.

They slowly let out the sail to **jibe**.

Set Sail!

Sailors check the weather before sailing. They stay in calm, well-known waters.

They always bring a
life jacket. Time to set sail!

Glossary

balance—the ability to stay upright

cruisers—sailboats used for long trips

dinghies—small, light sailboats often used by beginners

flares—bright lights used to signal to others or attract attention

jibe—to turn a sailboat by moving the sail from one side of the boat to the other

navigation—related to finding the way from place to place

points of sail—the directions a sailboat can travel in relation to the wind

rig—to set up a sailboat's sails and rigging

rigging—the system of ropes, wires, and cables used to control the sails

rudder—the part of a ship that steers

tack—to sail into the wind by moving in a zigzag motion

trim—to adjust sails to move in different winds

To Learn More

AT THE LIBRARY

Koran, Maria, and John Willis. *Sailboat.* New York, N.Y.: AV2, 2021.

Grack, Rachel. *Kayaking.* Minneapolis, Minn.: Bellwether Media, 2027.

Grack, Rachel. *Rowing.* Minneapolis, Minn.: Bellwether Media, 2027.

ON THE WEB

FACTSURFER

Factsurfer.com gives you a safe, fun way to find more information.

1. Go to www.factsurfer.com.
2. Enter "sailing" into the search box and click 🔍.
3. Select your book cover to see a list of related content.

Index

The images in this book are reproduced through the courtesy of: Capturas E, front cover (top), pp. 6-7; FamVeld, front cover (bottom), pp. 16, 21; Celso Pupo, p. 3; lunamarina, p. 4; DDurrich, pp. 4-5; Wangkun Jia, p. 5; Andrey, p. 7; CreativeSuburb, p. 8; Ilja, pp. 8-9; Pressmaster, pp. 10-11; sunday_morning, p. 11 (gloves); Mustafa, p. 11 (life jacket); Leo, p. 11 (flares); Vereshchagin Dmitry, p. 11 (sailboat); Tatiana Diuvbanova, pp. 12-13, 14; CasarsaGuru, p. 13; Paan Lily, pp. 16-17; Lena Ivanova, pp. 18-19; Kazakov, p. 19 (tack); vuk8691, p. 19 (jibe); mgstudyo, p. 19 (in irons); valio84sl, p. 19 (running); YanLev Alexey Sizov, pp. 20-21; Mai Groves, p. 23.